TELL ME

When You Are Tired of Me

  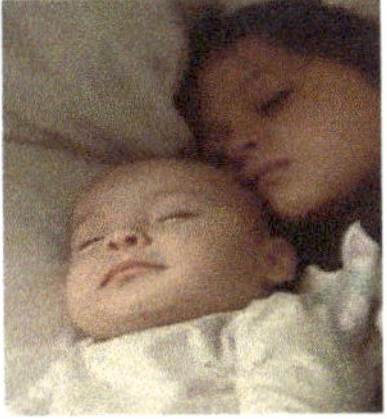

River Woods Writers & Dreamers
Mary & Michael

The River Woods Writers—Wauwatosa, WI
ISBN: 979-8-3305-6205-3
Title: *Tell Me When You Are Tired of Me*
Author: River Woods Writers & Dreamers Mary & Michael
Digital distribution | 2024
Paperback | 2024

Published in the United States by New Book Authors Publishing

Tell Me When You
Are Tired of Me

River Wood Writers & Dreamers
Mary & Michael

Dedication

To Bernice and Mary

—Having Become Friends—

The exquisite fabric of lives intertwined
Sequined with laughter shared
Dyed to subtle hues by mingled tear
A love wrap tailored by
"you're still mine" glances
Warmer than the coldest alone
Iridescent before life's darkest fear.
                    —Michael

◆◆◆◆◆

v

Table of Contents

◆◆◆◆◆

Introduction
—Children Are Sacred—

Children are Sacred—the manifestation of Divine Goodness and the embodiment of that Goodness at work in our world. This does not preclude whiney temper tantrums, smelly pants or hand prints on newly painted walls. It does mean, however, that, in unpredictable moments, instinct and events, children challenge us to seek transcendence. Their gift—a clear call to reach beyond the fingertips of our outstretched arms and enter into life's mystery in our world of apparent contradictions, failures, illusions and faulty perceptions.

Yes, children are sacred—sacred in their profound human potential. The potential to be all that we have as yet been unable to be. A potential, both simple and profound. The potential to dream and turn a stick into a rocket ship or a dandelion into an orchid. The potential to learn and to discover more than we ever thought possible. To unfold the mystery of why ants walk so fast or how people become tribes. They have within them capacities both common and profound—to hit a ball or run a race, to compose a symphony or a work of art, bringing alive the colors, textures and shapes of human experience on a plain white canvas.

Children are sacred in their innocence and trust, making them mirrors of the Divine and forcing us, in all honesty, to do better and be better than we ever thought attainable. Children, though powerless are still powerful, raising up to the surface burning sorrow at the sight of their suffering. And, in spite of their young failures and sometimes self-destructive choices, they force us to focus on the ways and means of creating a world built on diversity, integrity and respect—a vision untouched by hatred, injustice or prejudice. Children provide us with hope to imagine a better place to live and have courage to create a better future for us all.

In the face of their exuberance and imaginations, children stop us from living an all too hurried and harried existence, allowing us to be captivated by their presence. Too young to imagine a future beyond tomorrow, they teach us the joy and happiness of embracing each moment as it occurs in real time. In their midst, when we look into their heart-capturing eyes, we are given an opportunity to redeem our world from conflict and hate with open hearts—letting our spirits rise up with laughter and dance with delight

Within a child's small, fragile body lies the center of life's mysterious ability to be adaptable and resilient in the face of life's challenges and obstacles—to grow and develop the capacity to reach beyond the horizons of ordinary expectations. Children bear constant witness to that fact, offering endless testimony to compel us to realize and understand the human journey is not finished. Acknowledging we are merely works-in-progress. Never finished. Never complete. Merely travelers and sojourners across the landscape of earth.

Time's Signature

Over the Course
of Our Lives

Wondering

I sat staring into the evening's
darkening purple horizon,
Aware of a slow song...Hollow...
Empty of note or word
A sustaining echo of longing for something gone.

Wondering, I ask,

My Child will you love me when I am old?
When your strong arms lay hold of life
to shake from it adventure, knowledge and love,
I will rock, trying to remember.
Trying to remember and relish the days of
your finally becoming a Man.

Will your exuberance have time for patience?
Will your imagination have room for memories?
Will you take my hands and let me
feel your heart alive?

◆◆◆◆◆

The New York Times
Where Is Easter Island?
foldout map inside!
SOLAR SYSTEM

WORLD OF OUR FATHERS
IRVING HOWE
JACQUELINE KENNEDY
W.E.B. DU BOIS
ROBERT KENNEDY
EDWARD M. KENNEDY
Unbelievable   KATY TUR
THE MAKING OF MILWAUKEE
The Price of Loyalty
RON SUSKIND
BOBBY KENNEDY
CHRIS MATTHEWS
THE GREEK ISLES
JOSEPH CAMPBELL   THE MYTHIC IMAGE
ROYAL PALACES

On Teaching My Son How to Read

Come with me, my son,
while I introduce you to my friends, the words.

Shake hands with them and
they will take you to the land of imagination.

And discovery—
the land of the four legged and the winged.

My friends, the words,
will paint pictures of worlds beyond the stars
And lead your soul through the darkest night.

They will help keep
the sparkle of wonder in your eyes
And teach you to stand straight in the storm, While
tickling your spirit until it laughs out loud.

Then dry your tears with
the soft cloth of knowing you are not alone.

Come, My Son—
ride the words to the four corners of the earth. Find
the treasure house and mystery of being alive.

♦♦♦♦♦

Tell Me When You Are Tired of Me

I see you, little girl, peeking out
From behind your mother's leg.
Here is a magic gift for you.
It's ice cream that never melts.
A secret for the farthest corner
Of your private dresser drawer.
A forgotten doll never really lost.
An always new and shining penny.
This magic is for you to have
For always as your very own.
One last thing, my little friend—
I love you—and your mother too.

A Walk in the Park

Where are you going, my sunshine girl?
Where are you going, my sweetest dear?

Across the bridge to sunshine land?
To sparkles and shimmers?
And color matched swirls?

Where are you going, my sunshine girl?
Where are you going, my sweetest dear?

Across the bridge of freedom's light
And fulfillment's softest dreams?
To a land of together and dazzling bright light?
A land of shadows framed in uncertainty?
Or one where hands hold your heart?

Where have you gone, my sunshine girl
Where have you gone...

◆◆◆◆◆

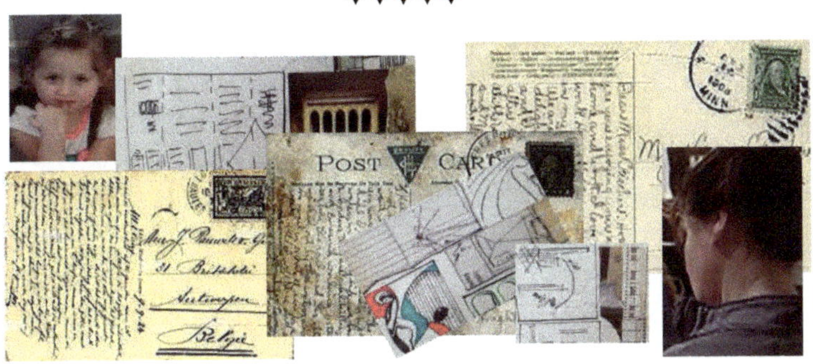

Amanda

So long ago and only yesterday,
You grew in my body and in my heart.
So long ago and only yesterday.
You were born from my body
And still abide more deeply in my heart.
With giggles and smiles,
With changings and late night feeding,
You stretched my heart wider
than I could imagine.

When the circle of seasons
reached only half the journey,
You slipped away.

In the dark of mystery and
the cold of not knowing,
I must believe the shining face of God
Startled you into eternity.

In the dark of mystery and the cold
of not knowing, I must believe
the tender hand of Jesus led you
Across the threshold to live with him
And still abide with me.

So long ago and only yesterday...

❖❖❖❖❖

The Tree

She told her secrets to the tree
That lived just outside her window.
Timid overtures in privacy
To secure a sympathetic ear—
Her ever present and constant companion.

On warm, summer afternoons,
Whenever she whispered its name,
It bent its branches down ever
Closer to the open window and
Lightly tapped on the wooden ledge.

Whether she spoke tentatively,
With her eyes swimming in tears,
Or confidently with words assertive and bold,
The Tree listened attentive with patience
to her every word, her every syllable.

Never distant, never far
A truly steady and reliable friend
Always kind and trustworthy,
It graced her little world
From just outside her window.

❖❖❖❖❖

The Vanity

No one ever saw her there.
Sitting with such quiet reverence
before her Mother's dressing table—
her special homage to a sacred ritual.
The poignant image reflected in the
light of a woman's vanity mirror—
a blue-eyed, freckle-faced little girl,
gazing in rapt attention at the sight
of her Mother's keepsake treasures.
Objects she had long since memorized
for the details of their charm and beauty.

Hand-made wisps of paper leaves
on top of an ornamental box of letters.
Standing guard over their presence,
Limoges porcelain figurines,
heads leaning into each other's—
Their hushed gesture, a whisper of secrets,
They watched lovingly over
a strand of lustrous pearls, peeking out
flirtatiously from beneath the cover
of its embroidered pink satin case.
A corsage of silk flowers lying nearby.

A little girl's eyes lingered in dream-like reverie,
captivated by the mysterious meaning attached

to their precious presence and valued importance.
Wanting to hold each object in the
palms of her hands, she was barely able
to resist the urge to caress every object with love—
Remembering instead, a dire warning not
to touch a single one of her Mother's treasures.
Instead, she let her awe and imagination
inform the question of her heart's desire—
"Will I be a lady as pretty as my Mother?"

The Dresser Drawer

Gramma, what do you hide
in your dresser drawer?

What do you mean, Child?

The second drawer, the big, wide one.

Oh, Child, that imagination of yours
is like a new puppy, runnin' all over the place.

No, I saw you when that big mirror
looked back at you
And you slid your hand into that drawer—
Your face got that look
like you was ready to tell a story—
that kinda serious smile and the shiny eyes—
then it was like somebody pulled
the shade on a sunny day.

Well, Child, I'll tell you so's
that imagination don't run wild.
But it has to be our secret.

Way back in the far corner
of the big old drawer is an envelop.
One of those flowery, four fold envelopes
all tied with a pretty bow.

Only your Gramma can touch that envelope.
Else everythin' in it will run away—
Memories will scoot off and hide.
A great big laugh will jump out
and fly away till everythin's quiet.
A tear will drop down and disappear in the rug.
There'll be a soft hand pass by
your cheek and be gone.
All at once all sorts of sights and sounds
will fly away to nowhere, all at once.

How come you hide all that stuff, Gramma?

Oh, Child, some days it is just
too much to carry and keeps getting in the way.
Someday I'll have time, then
I'll carefully take out that envelope and
gently set it on the table right here.
I'll ever so slowly pull on that bow and
unfold one side at a time. I'll sit here and smile.
Pretty soon my old heart'll get all warm
and start to do one of those slooow old folk dances
For a long long time.

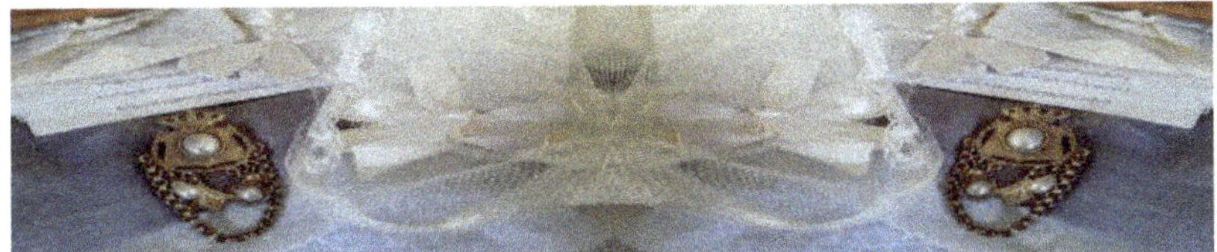

The Circus Child

I can…
        Touch the tip of my tongue to the end of my
            nose.
            Stand on one leg
            and roller skate backwards.
            Imitate the sound
            of a blank tube of toothpaste.
            Cross only one eye
            while the other looks forward.
When I grow up…
Will these tricks be enough?
Will I know what to do?
Will they carry me through?
Or, will I stumble and fumble,
        Tripping and falling all over the place?
                Or, will I know just enough to touch
        The tip of an angel's wing and soar high right up
            straight into the Heavens—

Singing and dancing with courageous abandon—
        Fearless and confident no punishment awaits.

✦✦✦✦✦

1 0 2 8
5 9 8
4
6 1 3 7

Age Eleven

One two three, you learned to climb a tree
While up above the ground you learned
To look around to see what might be found.
Four five six, we will simply have to nix.
They are now so far gone.
They count for less than a pawn.
Seven eight nine used to seem fine.
But from use they are so frayed.
They are worth nothing even in trade.
And now you have passed through ten
To where you have never been.
Eleven is the place that brings a smile to your face
New dreams come to stretch you tall
Far beyond whatever is too small.

The Cardboard Fortress

He stepped through a doorway
and passed beyond the boundaries
of an invisible, parallel world.
Into the filmy, sweet pleasures
of his memories from long ago,
he traveled back through time and space—
down a road's long, dusty stretch
to a room now bathed in faded
yellow and ivory-cream silhouettes.
Coming into focus, a young boy,
lying on his stomach in the center of frayed carpet.
Chin in hands, he was staring straight ahead
into the heart of a dream come true.

Nearby, disorderly trails of folded,
paper clippings, scissors and glue
were strewn carelessly beside stacks
of colored papers and a pile of
his Mother's old Sear's catalogues.
Standing on the floor in front
of his eyes, upright and proud,
the marvel of his accomplishment

—The Cardboard Fortress

An amazing feat, those lofty towers
and ramparts already lined with cannons
waiting patiently for the arrival of soldiers
to stand firmly in place and man the artillery.

Devilishly inspired, he lined up the
regiments of his two opposing forces,
standing at strict attention before him—
awaiting a special signal to advance
steadily across the field of battle.
Organized. Equipped. Prepared.
Primed to out-maneuver the enemy,
storm the gates and break down
the barriers of their armed defenses.
Raising his hand above his head,
he shouted out his orders decisively.
The impending chaos had begun—
determined soldiers opened fire.

Suddenly, a noisy distraction in the backyard.
A rowdy band of neighborhood mischief-makers
coming to change the course of his entire
best-laid afternoon battle plans—
They were off to find adventure, searching
the shoreline near Asylum Point Lighthouse—
hoping to discover a secret pirate's treasure trove
located somewhere near the water's edge.

Not taking "no" for an answer, they
insisted he come outside "right this minute"
and ride his bike with them out to the point.
Happily distracted by his friends,
he ran outside with eager anticipation—
letting the door slam shut behind him.

That summer's day slipped out of focus,
bringing back clearly into a viewer's sight
an architect's crisp, modern studio—
a room flooded in bright, natural light.
At his desk, a man is applying the final
details and flourishes to his latest design.
Displayed everywhere, awards, citations
And priceless models of past commissions.
Nearby, protected inside a glass case,
a tired, time-worn collectible, carefully
preserved under layers of fragile repairs.
A child's once-prized possession, still standing
tall and upright—**A Cardboard Fortress**.

A Younger Brother

My brother Marquis is like
a backward mirror for my memory.
He reminds me of the joy
when I discovered how to walk.
And to reach higher than my arms could go.
To get some big person's treasure from the shelf
And drag it down below.

He reminds me of the mystery —
the joy of learning colors and tasting carrots.
And wearing clothes that are cool.
He reminds me of the first time,
standing on my own,
As the whole world wobbled around me.

Thank you, God, for giving me arms
to hold and hug and help Marquis.
Thank you for giving me
a tickle spot in my heart so we can laugh.
Thank you for the strong place in my heart so
I can be patient with a tender place for me to cry.
Thank you, God, for my brother's hand
To hold forever.

✦✦✦✦✦

A Father's Hands

My Son, the Lord is your Shepherd
I will guide you in his way

My Son, the Lord is your Rock and Salvation
In his stead, I will guard and protect you
all the days of your life

My hand for you will be a Helper
My heart for you will be a Home
As you rise up in humble strength
To stand before the Lord

On Going to School

The late October morning sun
Stretches pale fingers across
The still sleeping lawn.
I eagerly mount my trusty Hiawatha bike—
Breath clouds give testimony to energetic pedaling.
A weaving, zig-zag trail follows Hiawatha
Across the sparkling, brittle, frosty grass.
The crunch of broken ice on street puddles
Punctuates the morning stillness.

❖❖❖❖❖

My First Bike—A Gift From Grandpa

A Boy & Baseball

Once upon a time in a land far away. Well, actually not that long ago and not that far away, there was a young boy who really enjoyed playing baseball. He was a markedly ordinary child, much to the delight of his mother. And, like all boys his age, his world stretched to the farthest edges of his vivid imagination. All it took was a little sunshine, a ball and some wide open space. Out of that raw material he could easily fabricate bases loaded, bottom of the ninth, and a three-two count with the game on the line. He could be batter or pitcher, maybe both at the same time.

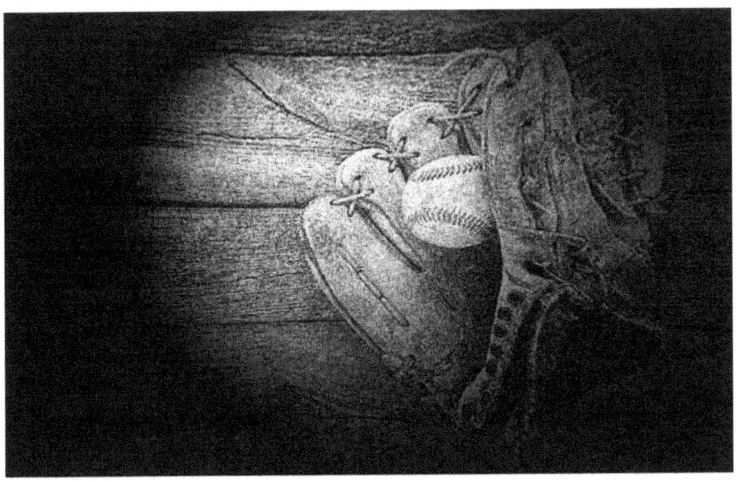

Well, back to my story. The day was hot. The sky stretched its generous, blue roof overhead. Here and there randomly scattered clouds wandered aimlessly. It was a lucky day. There was a bat, a ball, several friends, enough gloves to go around and a large empty field.

The batter called out the situation—bottom of the second, runners on first and third, one out. Ah, this was the time to go for the fence! The tension was on. The pitcher threw a fast ball straight towards him. Calculating speed, leverage and angle all at once, he swung hard. Crack! Lobbing the ball three feet in the air brought on all the fun! Off into the sun drenched summer sky, it exploded through the air. Friends' heads lurched skyward and squinted in the sun. They turned and ran—at first chasing, then settling into a slow glove-pounding trot until ball and glove met each other in a distinct slap. Runners hold. Next batter.

And so it went, more engaging in the imagination than in reality. As the innings passed, the sun got hotter and hotter. Shirts were discarded.

And, although sweaty hands made the bat slippery, that fact did nothing to dampen their adolescent enthusiasm. Barely developed arm muscles flexed often in their effort to hasten the arrival of manhood. Imagination worked its wonder here, too. A slight bump in the bicep morphed into a Ted Kluzewski power laden arm—a proud moment in the life of a young teen looking forward to becoming a man!

Time did not pass. It just stood still out of respect for the boyhood universe. But then, at some point, a distraction forced its way into the world of imagination. A shifting wind blew open a "refrigerator door." The damp cool breeze from Lake Superior rushed across the open field— sending the sun warmed air scrambling in rapid retreat. When the wind shifted, the long fly balls shrunk into lazy pop-ups. The sweat on hands and brow dried and cooled.

"Where's my shirt?"

This was enough to call for a quick consultation. In a beginning-to-shiver huddle, we reached a unanimous decision. Game called due to weather. We headed for home and a warm jacket, pledging to resume our dream on the morro— weather permitting.

Timeless Ten

I used to be able to make time stand still. I would take my baseball glove, a tennis ball and step outside at the front porch. In a moment, those three concrete steps morphed into county stadium. Right from the opening pitch, blazed against the steps, the game unfolded in an endless string of strategic moments:

Bottom of the third, nobody out, runner on first—with a well-placed pitch comes a fast return bounce, a swipe of the glove and quick throw back toward the steps—double play!! Warren Spahn, Johnny Logan, Joe Adcock all present in the blink of an eye.

The next pitch was bases loaded, top of the sixth. A sharp line drive snatched out of the air with a cat-quick glove. Disaster averted. Play after play unfolded, each a game changing moment, freed from the tyranny of sequence and filled with the thrill of an imagined moment. How many innings? Who knows. Never reaching the bottom of the ninth, only "game postponed" by the call to supper.

Oh, there were interruptions to the game. When the pitch produces a foul tip which crashes loudly against the aluminum front door. This draws a shouted response from my sister inside the house, "Be careful, you're going to break the window!"

In utter self-assurance, I deliver the next pitch to make a soft popup easily and safely corralled in my glove.

Pitch after pitch, the game goes on, inning and situation to disconnected inning and situation. The pitches, the catches, the relay throws all in a timeless, loosely connected world of their own.

After supper there may be time for some extra innings!

✦✦✦✦✦

The Big Fish

You can see the fish
And you can see my ear-to-ear grin.
But you can't see how deep it goes
Way down inside to the tip of my toes.

My Gramma is proud of me, you know.

I will show the picture a thousand times
Maybe even make up some rhymes.

Because my Gramma's proud of me.

No matter how many times
I tell the tale,
The endings the same, without fail.

Did I mention to you
My Gramma is really proud of me!!

Winter on Ray Nesser Pl

The evening air was crisp and cold. The snow was perfect. And she was in her glory—playing outside after dark with the big kids. A spunky three-year-old totally oblivious to the fact that she was there only because her big sister, Kay, was best friends with bossy Bonnie Brueckner—the undisputed leader of the neighborhood kids on Ray Nesser Pl.

Part charmer, part bully, she was now completely preoccupied organizing all the other kids into two groups in order to finish building snow forts on either side of the Brueckner's front yard. She was very busy impatiently ordering everyone else around. Who should be doing what and where they should be doing it. Some, digging fast and furious to carve out defensive positions in the growing mounds of hard-packed snow. Others, gathering together huge stockpiles of icy snowballs—artillery for the big snowball fight about to commence the moment everything was ready to go.

Suddenly, from behind her, off to one side, a flush of streaming, bright light spread its glow over a yard of white, glistening snow. Holding the porch door open against the cold, one of the neighborhood Dads called out loud and clear, "Joanie, it's time for you to come inside now."

"But, Daddy, I don't wanna come in now. You didn't call Kay to come in. Why can't I stay out with her and the big kids? We're gonna have a snowball fight pretty soon."

A Dad's irritated voice stated firmly and flatly, "Joanie, do I have to remind you that you are not a big kid? When you're Kay's age, you'll get your chance to stay out as late as she can. But until then, you'll have to come in when it's time for the little kids to come home. And that means you. No argument."

She knew it was useless to argue with her dad. That familiar, set tone of voice meant he was done talking—his words were now absolute.

She started heading for her house, but at a pace that more resembled a snail's sluggish crawl than that of a energetic little girl. She was definitely not happy and it showed. Jealous of the privilege her older sister's first-born status had afforded her, she held her lips pursed tightly—a reflection of her extreme annoyance over life's inevitable unfairness. Something she was just beginning to learn, but still much too young, unrelenting, and stubborn to give up without a struggle.

That three and a half-year-old was too busy pouting to notice her dad watching and waiting patiently for her at the door. She didn't see his face soften as he watched his youngest daughter crossing their yard. He guessed what she must be thinking about. How unfair she thought life was and how angry she was about it. Unknown to her, he was, at that moment, remembering how it had been for him, too, growing up with an older sister and brother, whose steps he was continually forced to follow throughout the course of his own childhood.

Then, just as she got inside the porch door, someone suddenly shouted out, "Fire away!"

She turned around at once to see all the kids yelling and screaming at the top of their lungs. The snowball fight had begun! Under a steady barrage of flying white snow, each group was defending their positions. It was a free-for-all—

impossible to predict who would win. And she could clearly see how much fun they were having. Anxious to find out who would win, she decided to make one more pleading attempt to her dad—hoping against hope, he might still relent and let her stay on the porch to see how it all ends.

But, when she turned back, she saw a look of horror on her dad's face. All of a sudden he cried out sharply, "Markie, what are you doing up there?!"

Without a moment's hesitation, he ran straight into the house, inadvertently letting the door close behind him. She stood there a minute in shock until it dawned on her that her baby brother must have gotten himself into trouble. He was always trying to climb up somewhere or other—a distinct personality trait that caused her mother to worry over him constantly during his waking hours. He was a handful and had to be watched every minute of every hour he was awake.

It dawned on her, standing there alone, that this particular incident might be for her a truly unexpected lucky break to stay on the porch after all. The timing couldn't be better. Now, there was no one to prevent her from watching the big kids finish their snowball fight. That is—until her dad discovered she hadn't followed him into the house and came looking for her.

"Oh well" she thought to herself, "at least, I will be able to watch some of it."

To get a better view of the action, she walked over to one of the windows at the other end of the porch. The street lights lite up the action perfectly. She kept looking for Kay in the mess of confusion, but couldn't see her clearly. By this time almost everyone was covered in snow. Gary Brueckner, Bonnie's brother, was pushing someone off a mound of snow in a vain effort to become "king of the hill." His opponent, a much bigger and stronger boy, had the decisive edge. She muffled her giggles and laughed into her mittens so no one inside the house would hear her. She didn't like Gary.

Then, just as she was taking her mitten away from her mouth, a passing headlight from a car turning onto the street reflected an unusual pattern on the icy window pane. It was something she had never noticed before—finely etched trails of frosted feathery swirls—like parades of lacey ribbons, unfurling their beauty across the window's surface. Mesmerized by their appearance and in spite of the cold, she took off one of her mittens. Using her fingernail like a pencil, she traced the subtle outlines of their delicate patterns—up to and down to, then sideways along, until she had explored every inch of their patterned existence from one end to the other.

Suddenly, out of nowhere, the awareness of an eerie, cold silence descended all around her. Startled, she awakened instantly from her trance-like state and quickly looked out the window—only to discover the street lights were on, but no kids were anywhere in sight. Frightened and confused, her mind immediately raced on ahead in a frantic effort to figure out what had happened. Where was Kay? How could she have come in without my seeing or hearing her? Did she just walk past me in the dark?? Didn't she see me here, or was she just ignoring me on purpose?? Oh I'll be in trouble now!

Panic-stricken, she immediately ran over to the house door and started to turn the knob. Pushing and pulling as hard as she could, but it wasn't turning at all. To her horrified surprise, it was locked.

Terrified by a chilling fear that gripped the very marrow of her bones, she suddenly let go of the handle and desperately started pounding her little fists as hard as she could against the door.

"Mommy, Mommy, Mommy." Her little body becoming increasingly racked with uncontrollable sobs.

To her overwhelming joy and relief, the door opened quickly. Her Mother, stunned by surprise, barely had just enough time to get out the words, "Joanie, what on earth?" before her terrified daughter rushed headlong into her arms.

Without a moment's hesitation, her mother scooped up her distraught little daughter into her arms, hugging and holding her tightly. The little girl's fear vanished at once when she felt the warmth of her mother's hug and heard that familiar comforting voice whisper in her ear, "Oh, Joanie, you're Ok now."

✦✦✦✦✦

43

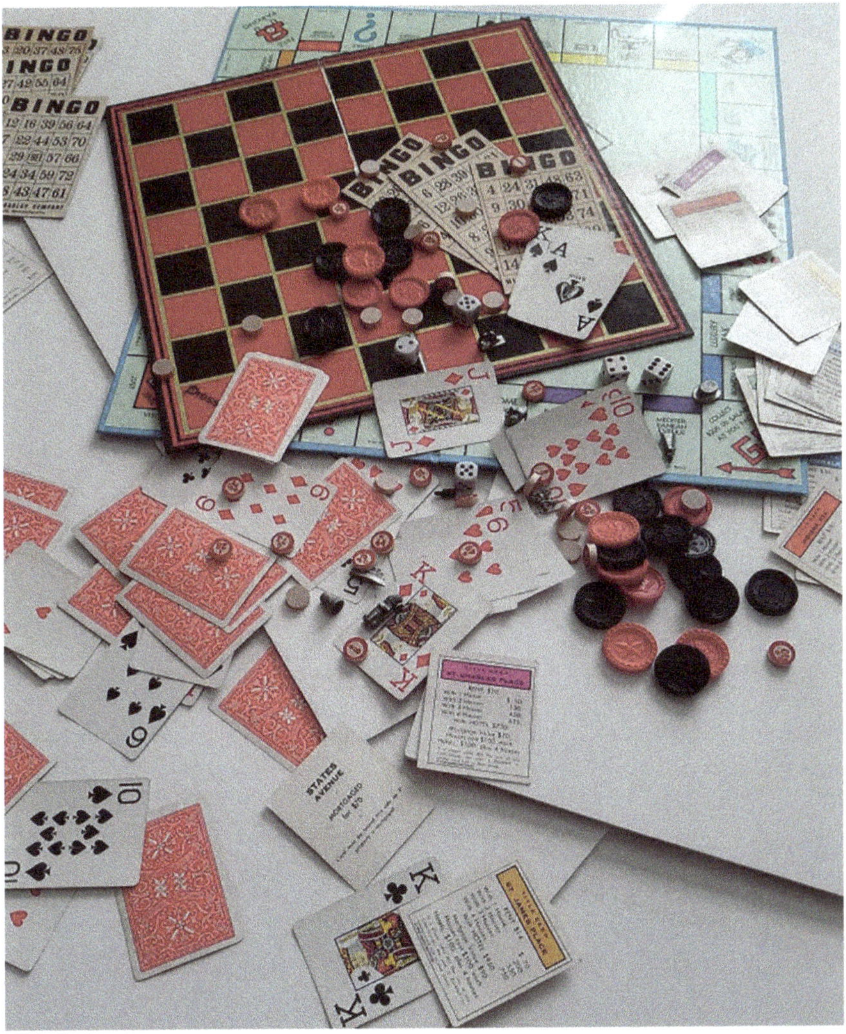
BINGO
STATES AVENUE
MORTGAGED for $75

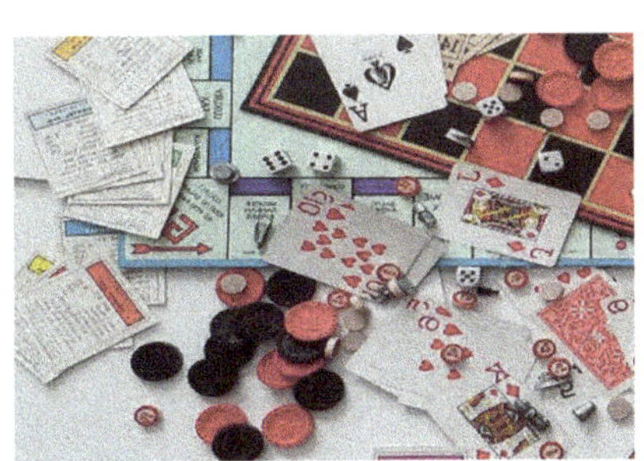

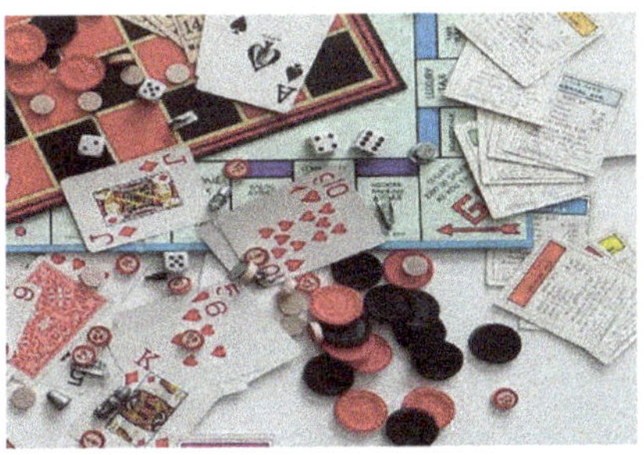

Sunday Afternoon Board Games

Shake up the dice
In a round plastic cup.
Toss them over the board
Climb up a ladder.
Then pick the wrong card
Your headed for jail.
Give the right answer
Become head of the class.
If you found a clue
Who did the crime?

Sunday afternoon fun
For a family of five.
Everyone's happy.
Everything's fine.
Until your brother
Gloats a little too long over
The joy of his winning
And you suddenly flip
Over the game board
Right on top of his head!

✦✦✦✦✦

The Dream Maker

Every so often,
on the day before yesterday,
while a little girl napped
alone in her room,
wisps of itinerant smoke
seeped through the cracks
of an old wooden floor—
announcing the pending arrival
of her Never-Seen Guest.

Ostentatiously dressed
in unsynchronized shades,
he mimicked the conventions
of the colors he wore.
Scalloped stripes streaming over
bright, wide polka dots.
Magentas and yellows
all mixed up together—
Over-done, over-dyed, overly dressed.

Balanced precariously
on a blind, spinning top,
three times on a ring,
he jumped up and down.
Then snapping his fingers
up in the air, he produced out of
nowhere, his mixed bag of tricks—

a comedy of errors all tied up together
with curling ribbons and a big satin bow.

Stupidly clowning
on an unsteady stage,
he slyly pulled on one end of his cuff.
In the breath of an instant,
his magical bag spun around,
tipping out in slow motion
sparkles of shimmering light
that floated down effortlessly
towards a little girl's toes.

The nearer they came
to the foot of the bed,
strange transformations
began to take place.
A rainbow of colors and shapes,
like waves of musical drifts,
flowed gently up over her head—
protecting a little girl's slumber
with the warmth of a tender caress.

Once past the scribbles
of his hypnotic doodles,
his work now complete,
an expression of joy spread
its glow all over his face.

The lions and tigers had
been vanquished at last—
no longer allowed to prey

upon a little girl's dreams.
Pleased and elated,
he spun around on his heels.
Spreading the tips of his fingers wide open,
he let fly the flourish of his finishing touch—
a spray of dazzling, white stars
strewn from one end to the next.
Then suddenly, he turned abruptly and
leapt out of sight, never seen, never noticed—
As quick as he came, he was gone.

❖❖❖❖❖

50

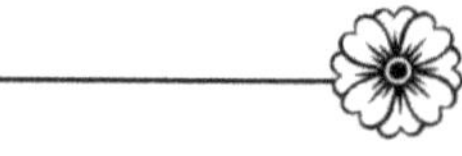

Discovery

In all God's universe, one possession is most dear,
A small plain box, quite ordinary—yet. oh
What treasures lies beneath its lid!
Quite ordinary things of days and
weeks and years gone by.
A teddy bear with one eye—
the other lost when one bright light
exploded into a thousand stars.
A cowboy without his rope in hand,
Sitting upright on his three legged steed—
Having tied wild passion with too frail a cord.
A bent and ragged deck of playing cards—
Testimony to frequent grand designs
left scattered by a breeze.
A broken mirror reflecting fragmented dreams.
All memories of times and places
where here and now was not enough.
Memories where Mercy's Hand reached
Into nowhere to make it a home.
All these memories of human and divine lie
safely stored in that sacred box called me.

✦✦✦✦✦

Epilogue
—Through the Mystery of the Universe—

God's Shadow-Speak

✦✦✦✦✦

Thank you, Dear God, for both your presence
and your absence in shadows.
Silent words declaring,
"I'm here and there and not either" —
somehow both at once.
The soft emergence of dawn's shadows
declares your presence in gentle determination.
Noon day's shadows forcefully announce
You are beyond without being absent.
Sunset's growing, long-deepening shadows
under painted skies of majesty and grandeur
speak a promise of peaceful rest.
Even the scurrying shadow of a windswept cloud
declares the truth of your respectful presence—
rushing and still, all at once.
Consistently, into my laboring dullness,
you speak a shadow word of startling awareness—
a deepening mystery which makes
the familiar oh so different.
If only I allow my spirit to stand still and
absorb your shadow-speak,
I will know your presence.

✦✦✦✦✦

About the River Woods Writers

✦✦✦✦✦

As Mary and Michael became better acquainted over time, they discovered they each had a deep and abiding love of expressing, through words and pictures, the Mystery and Wonder found in the ordinary "stuff" of life. Each of them saw in each other a person who was indeed someone, who wanted to "stand still" and experience the joy of meeting the Mystery and Wonder as it was living in the quiet moments of the ordinary.

From this common understanding immerged a desire to share the experience of being present to life's wonder and mystery in what is so often taken for granted. First, they shared their own individual works with each other and second, they found a way to do so with others by combining their creative talents and skills—believing the telling makes the reality of the experience even more true in the telling, even more real in the sharing.

The pages of the book are their invitation to the reader to take a walk along "The River Woods." Each poem and photograph was offered with this thought in mind, "Here, take what we have found, enjoy and savor it."

✦✦✦✦✦

Acknowledgements
—Book Production Design & Production—

No book is ever brought into The Light of Day without special attention and consideration being paid to the specific graphic design details that go into the final public presentation of the work itself—details, that, when successful, not only enhance the overall quality, and beauty of the work, but also create in the public's minds and hearts a positive perception of the book's true meaning and purpose. As The River Woods Writers, in using our own skills in photography and graphic design, we hope we have been successful in this endeavor.

Mary:
Cover & Book Page Layout design—Mary
All Story & Poetry Still Life Photographic Art
Imaging Introduction—Panoramic Landscape Photographs, *Summer & Fall*
Epilogue: Four Seasons Photographs, **Summer & Fall**

Michael:
Introduction: Four Seasons, **Winter, Spring, Summer & Fall**—Close-up Views.
Panoramic Landscape Photographs: **Winter & Spring**
Contributing Photographs for Stories: *The Big Fish, On Going To School, A Boy & Baseball, Timeless Ten, Winter On Ray Nesser Pl*
Epilogue: Four Seasons, **Winter & Spring**

❖❖❖❖❖

—A SPECIAL THANK YOU—

✦✦✦✦✦

No acknowledgements are complete without mentioning the special contribution of others, whose talents and gifts have made, I believe, a significant contribution to highlighting the beauty of children in our lives. At this time, I wish to express my deep appreciation to Jeri Kaufman for contributing photos for both the **Tell Me** book cover spread and Michael's poems, **Amanda** and **A Younger Brother**. In my opinion, they strengthen the meaning and relevancy of Tell Me When You Are Tired of Me in our Time and Space.

✦✦✦✦✦

58

RIVER WOODS
WRITERS&DREAMERS

MARY&MICHAEL

TELL ME

When You Are Tired of Me

www.ingramcontent.com/pod-product-compliance
Lightning Source LLC
Chambersburg PA
CBHW041153150726

48006CB00015B/1976